UNSOLVED MYSTERIES

The D. B. Cooper Hijacking

BY TOM STREISSGUTH

Published by The Child's World®
1980 Lookout Drive • Mankato, MN 56003-1705
800-599-READ • www.childsworld.com

ACKNOWLEDGMENTS
The Child's World®: Mary Berendes, Publishing Director
Red Line Editorial: Editorial direction
The Design Lab: Design
Amnet: Production

DESIGN ELEMENT: Shutterstock Images

PHOTOGRAPHS ©: C. Paul Fell/iStockphoto, cover; I. Cholakov/iStock-
photo, 6; AP Images, 7; John Brueske/Shutterstock Images, 10;
Shutterstock Images, 12, 17; Bettmann/Corbis, 15, 20; HO/Reuters/
Corbis, 19; Purestock/Thinkstock, 23

ISBN 9781634070720
LCCN 2014959762

Printed in the United States of America
Mankato, MN
July, 2015
PA02266

ABOUT THE AUTHOR

Tom Streissguth has written more
than 100 biographies, histories, and
geography books for young readers.
Streissguth publishes journalism
collections for students, teachers,
researchers, and libraries. He lives in
Woodbury, Minnesota.

TABLE OF CONTENTS

THE PASSENGER IN SUNGLASSES

It was a rainy, cold evening in 1971. A Northwest Airlines 727 jet flew over the mountains. Rivers ran through thick forests more than 10,000 feet (3,048 m) below.

A door on the plane was open. A man stood on the lowered **aft** stairs. He had on a raincoat and a parachute. A bundle of cash was strapped to his body. The money amounted to $200,000.

The jet was flying at 170 miles per hour (274 kph). The man held on to the rail. He looked down into the night. Then he jumped.

Checking In

Hours earlier, the man had walked calmly through the Portland, Oregon, airport. He wore sunglasses, a black suit, and a skinny tie. He carried a small briefcase.

It was the day before Thanksgiving. Travelers crowded the big **terminal**. They checked their bags. Then they waited for their planes. Everyone had somewhere to go.

A ticket agent waited at the counter. The man in sunglasses bought a ticket to Seattle, Washington. He gave his name as Dan Cooper. The flight was leaving soon. The fare was only $20.

Cooper boarded the plane. Seat 18C was waiting. It was an aisle seat in an empty row. He placed his briefcase on the seat beside him.

With a roar, the 727 jet rose into the air. The flight would last less than an hour.

MYTH OR FACT?
Dan Cooper used a hat as a disguise.

This is a myth. After Cooper hijacked the plane, artists drew sketches of him. The sketches appeared in newspapers. Some show a man with straight dark hair. In others, Cooper wears a **homburg** hat. In fact, Cooper had no hat or other headgear.

Dan Cooper boarded a 727 passenger plane similar to this one.

Gone with the Wind

Dan Cooper waved to a flight attendant. He handed her a note. The note demanded $200,000 and two parachutes. He wanted to receive the **ransom** in Seattle. If he did not receive it, the note said, he would destroy the plane with a bomb.

The plane landed in Seattle. Local police brought the money and parachutes. The other passengers got off. Cooper directed the pilots to fly to Reno, Nevada. He told them to fly at a low airspeed. He wanted them to keep the landing gear down. The plane took off. Cooper was the only passenger.

The crew aboard the 727 spoke to reporters after the Cooper hijacking.

Soon, the pilots saw a warning light. It showed that a cabin door was open. The plane dipped slightly. Cooper had lowered the aft stairs. As instructed, the pilots stayed in the **cockpit**. They continued to fly to Reno.

Two hours after Cooper lowered the aft stairs, the pilots landed the plane. They had reached Reno. The pilots hurried back to the cabin. Cooper was gone. So was one parachute and the money. All that remained was the other parachute and a skinny black tie.

The Federal Bureau of Investigation (FBI) began to investigate. Their search continues to this day. The **hijacking** is the only unsolved case of air piracy in U.S. history.

CHAPTER TWO

THE LANDING ZONE

Police radios buzzed with the news of the hijacking. Reporter Clyde Jabin heard the story. He called the FBI. Did they have a suspect?

An FBI agent replied, "D. Cooper." But Jabin did not hear the name accurately. He wrote down "D. B. Cooper." Jabin's report on the hijacking was the first to reach the public. People knew the suspect as D. B. Cooper, not Dan Cooper.

The FBI did not correct the mistake. They knew it would help their investigation. Clues that turned up about "Dan Cooper" would be useful.

Anyone claiming to know "D. B. Cooper" would probably not have good information. The agents would follow clues linked to the right name.

Mapping the Jump

While the hijacking was in progress, other pilots tried to find the plane. But it was difficult to track. Its cabin lights were off. The sky was dark.

After Cooper jumped, the FBI estimated his location. He probably jumped between 8:11 p.m. and 8:16 p.m. He would have landed near Ariel, Washington. This town lies along Lake Merwin. To the south is the Columbia River. The possible landing zone covered about 25 square miles (65 sq km).

Helicopters hovered above the slopes. Search teams scrambled through forests. FBI agents knocked on doors and stopped drivers. They asked for information. Agents scanned the area for a parachute **canopy**. Few found useful clues. Clouds and cold weather slowed the search.

Cooper probably landed near the Columbia River in Washington.

Reporters and airline workers also searched for Cooper. Northwest Airlines offered a reward of $25,000 for information. The *Seattle Post-Intelligencer* newspaper offered $5,000.

More people joined the hunt. They drove to Ariel. Many climbed hills and scanned treetops. They searched riverbanks. Few people found any evidence.

Continuing the Search

The FBI looked for other clues. They checked the parachutes given to Cooper. One was a Pioneer brand parachute with arm and leg straps. The other was an older military parachute. It was harder to steer.

Cooper used the military parachute. The FBI saw this as an important clue. The hijacker may have been in the military. Perhaps he was a **paratrooper**. Most skydivers would use the safer Pioneer.

Cooper's airplane knowledge was another clue. He may have been a pilot. Cooper knew things about the 727 that most people don't know. He knew that the aft stairs could be lowered while the plane was in flight. He also knew ways to keep the plane's airspeed down. This knowledge helped him hijack the plane.

MYTH OR FACT?
Cooper's parachute has been found.

Many experts believe this is true. In 2008, children found a parachute in Cooper's landing zone. It was torn and faded. They brought it to the police. Experts studied the parachute. It matched descriptions of Cooper's parachute. It had been lying in place for many years.

Military paratroopers have experience jumping out of planes.

Where did the hijacker get the name Dan Cooper? Agents knew it was not his real name. The name was probably from a comic book called *Dan Cooper*. This comic book was published in Belgium in 1954. The fictional Cooper flew in the Canadian Air Force. He was a skilled skydiver. In one comic, a kidnapper demands ransom money.

The comic book was written in French. Agents believed the hijacker had visited Europe. He may have read French. Agents tried to match clues to suspects. But they never proved Cooper's identity.

In 1972, agents hunted through the Oregon wilderness again. Two hundred soldiers helped them in this search. They found a body. Tests showed it was not Dan Cooper.

Some agents believed Cooper did not survive the jump. Jumping from a plane, even with a good parachute, is dangerous. If Cooper survived, he was probably injured.

No body or clothing was ever found. Nobody could be sure about what happened. But years later, some of the ransom money mysteriously appeared.

MYTH OR FACT?
A volcano covered the search area with ash.

This is a myth. In 1980, Mount St. Helens erupted. A huge cloud of ash rose into the sky. Cooper's landing zone was northwest of the volcano. Did the ash destroy clues? In fact, the ash blew east, not west. Only a very thin layer of ash reached the landing zone.

CHAPTER THREE

THE MISSING MONEY

It was a pleasant day in 1980. The Ingram family was visiting Tena Bar, a **sandbar** in Oregon. Brian Ingram was digging in the sand. Nearby, the Columbia River flowed.

Something was buried in the sand. Brian dug deeper. He pulled out bundles of money. The bundles held $20 bills. The cash was dirty and worn. It was covered with silvery sand.

In all, there was $5,800. The bills were faded and torn. The Ingrams took the money to an FBI office. Agents checked the **serial numbers**

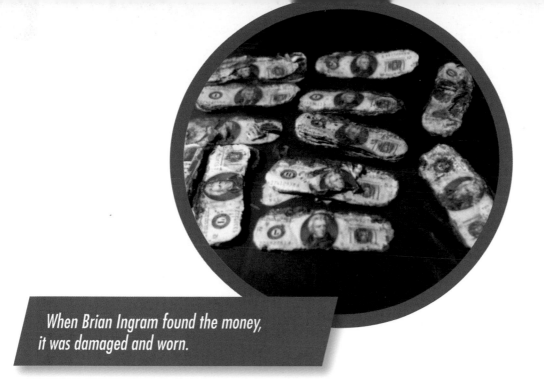

When Brian Ingram found the money,
it was damaged and worn.

on the bills. They had a record of the serial numbers on Cooper's ransom money. The numbers matched. Brian Ingram had found some of Cooper's buried treasure.

A Strange Treasure

Tena Bar is on the north bank of the Columbia River. Cooper's flight followed a path several miles to the east. The sandbar lies 40 miles (64 km) south of Cooper's landing zone. How did the money get there?

The money could have drifted along a smaller river or stream. Or perhaps someone had hidden the money there.

Tena Bar is not a good place to bury treasure. The sand shifts with the wind. Sooner or later, buried things reach the surface. Often, visitors dig into the sandbar. In 1974, **dredging** machines had cleared a channel in the river. The machines dug sand from the bottom of the river. They dumped the sand on Tena Bar.

Agents checked the site. They could not find any other money. They also checked dredging records. The cash sat on top of a layer of clay. The 1974 dredging had pushed the clay to this spot. The money had gotten there after 1974.

Rubber bands held the money together. They offered another clue. When left outside, rubber bands weaken. If they are stretched, they eventually break. It does not take long. Usually, the bands break in less than a year. But the rubber bands on the found money were still intact. Someone likely buried the money shortly before Brian

Ingram found it. This person chose Tena Bar, in 1979 or 1980. Who was it? Why?

FBI agents still keep a list of the serial numbers on the ransom money. Many authorities believe that Cooper never spent it. So far, no one else has come forward with a true Dan Cooper bill.

FBI agents use serial numbers to identify currency bills.

CHAPTER FOUR

SUSPECTS

Through the years, the FBI continued its search. Shortly after the hijacking, FBI agents sent out a bulletin. They gave a witness's description of Cooper. He was a white male in his mid-forties. He was close to 6 feet (1.8 m) tall. Cooper had brown hair and brown eyes.

A sketch of Cooper also went out. It showed a man with dark eyes and plain features. Another sketch showed Cooper in sunglasses.

To some, D. B. Cooper was a hero. They were amazed that someone could escape the FBI for so long. D. B. Cooper songs and books appeared.

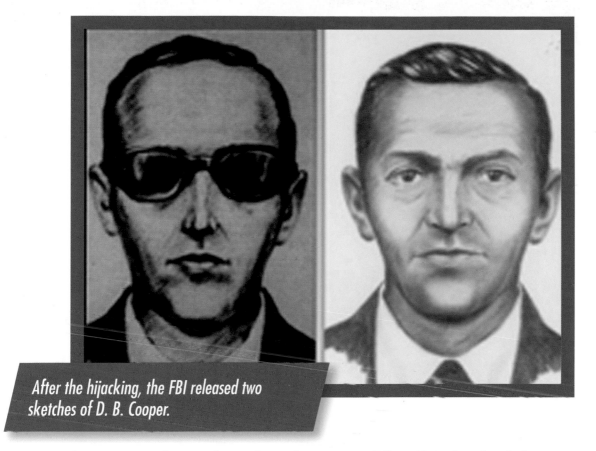

Some people confessed to the crime. The FBI checked their stories. They ruled them all out.

Copycats and Possible Suspects

Similar hijackings followed. Richard McCoy was an army veteran. In April 1972, he boarded a 727 in Denver. He ordered the pilots to fly to San Francisco. He demanded $500,000 in ransom. The plane took off again. McCoy jumped out over Utah. Like Cooper, McCoy used a parachute to escape. Police caught him two days later. McCoy was carrying a bag of money when he was arrested. He was sentenced to 45 years in prison. Soon after he was sentenced, McCoy escaped. FBI agents found him in Virginia Beach, Virginia. They killed him in a shootout.

Some people think McCoy and Cooper were the same person. But McCoy was only 29 in 1972. Cooper was probably much older. Perhaps McCoy was imitating Cooper's methods. Others tried the same plan. Fifteen similar hijackings took place

On April 9, 1972, police arrested Richard McCoy for hijacking a plane.

in 1972. The FBI or police caught every copycat. Only Cooper escaped the lawmen.

There are other men who might be Dan Cooper. Kenneth Christiansen trained as an army paratrooper. He knew a lot about planes. Christiansen died in 1994 at the age of 68. After he died, his family found nearly $200,000 in his bank account. No one knew how he had gotten the money.

Duane Weber was also an army veteran. Before he died in 1995, he confessed to being Dan Cooper. In 1979, he had traveled to the Columbia River. He visited Tena Bar. Later, Brian Ingram found the ransom money in the same spot.

The FBI did not declare Christiansen or Weber official suspects. They cannot match evidence from Cooper's plane to anyone. More searches have taken place. Few other clues were found. Today, the case remains unsolved. The mystery of D. B. Cooper continues.

MYTH OR FACT?
The FBI tested Cooper's DNA.

This is a fact. DNA is a chemical code in the body's cells. Every person's DNA is different. Police gather DNA samples from crime scenes. They use the samples to identify criminals. FBI agents pulled DNA samples from Cooper's tie. However, they have not found a DNA match.

Glossary

aft (AFT) The aft is the rear of a ship or an airplane. The hijacker climbed onto the aft stairs.

canopy (CAN-uh-pee) A canopy is the upper part of a parachute. The canopy drifted into the treetops before the skydiver reached the ground.

cockpit (KAHK-pit) The cockpit of a plane is a small cabin where pilots fly. The copilot left the cockpit to check on the passengers.

dredging (DREJ-ing) Dredging is digging out sand and rocks from the bottom of a river. The dredging operation cleared a channel through the riverbed.

hijacking (HYE-jak-ing) During a hijacking, a person steals or takes control of a vehicle. The D. B. Cooper case is the only unsolved plane hijacking in the United States.

homburg (HAHM-berg) A homburg is a type of men's hat with a wide brim. Some people thought that D. B. Cooper wore a homburg hat.

paratrooper (PA-ruh-troop-er) A paratrooper is a member of the military trained in parachute jumping. Some people think D. B. Cooper was a paratrooper.

ransom (RAN-suhm) Ransom is money demanded during a hijacking. D. B. Cooper asked for a ransom of $200,000.

sandbar (SAND-bar) A sandbar is a ridge of sand lying near a beach or rising from a riverbank. Brian Ingram was digging into a sandbar when he found bundles of money.

serial numbers (SIHR-ee-ul NUM-burz) Serial numbers are numbers used to identify currency bills. The FBI kept track of the serial numbers on the money given to Cooper.

terminal (TUR-muh-null) A terminal is a building where passengers board and exit planes. Before a holiday, an airport terminal is often crowded.

To Learn More

BOOKS

Boyer, Crispin. *That's Sneaky: Stealthy Secrets and Devious Data That Will Test Your Lie Detector.* Chicago: National Geographic Society, 2014.

MacDonald, Beverley. *It's True: Crime Doesn't Pay.* Toronto: Annick Press, 2006.

Schroeder, Andreas. *Thieves! True Stories from the Edge.* Toronto: Annick Press, 2005.

WEB SITES

Visit our Web site for links about D. B. Cooper: **childsworld.com/links**

Note to Parents, Teachers, and Librarians: We routinely verify our Web links to make sure they are safe and active sites. So encourage your readers to check them out!

Index